Implementing Linked Lists

Solving Complex Coding Challenges

Table of Contents

Chapter 1. Introduction

Special Report: "Implementing Linked Lists: Solving Complex Coding Challenges"

Welcome to an unpretentious, hands-on exploration of one of the foundational structures in computer science, the Linked List. This Special Report is designed to unravel the work behind often complex and challenging coding problems associated with the implementation of this fundamental data structure. The discourse has been encapsulated thoughtfully to suit coders of all levels, keeping it as grounded as possible in its explanation of concepts so that they don't seem like an abstract distant reality. We understand that delving into coding challenges can seem like a daunting task, yet with this report, you'll find that beauty and logic behind these complex problems can make your journey truly fascinating. Look forward to empowering yourself, simplifying your coding approach, and becoming a stronger problem solver. The understanding gained from this comprehensive guide will prove beneficial whether you're just starting, or preparing for intricate problem solving tests. Embrace your curiosity and let's decode complex coding challenges together!

Chapter 2. Understanding Linked Lists: A Foundation

Linked lists serve as one of the cornerstones of data structures within computer science. Their understanding paves the way towards grasifying more complex structures and plays an integral part in solving numerous coding challenges.

To begin with, think of a linked list as a chain of nodes, whereby each node contains data and a reference (or link) to the next node in the sequence. This fundamental structure allows for efficient insertions and deletions, which might not be possible in other linear data structures like arrays. Let's delve into the specifics.

2.1. The Basic Structure

Every linked list is formed by nodes, which are the fundamental units of this data structure. A node is typically composed of two parts: the data part and the link part. The data part stores the information, while the link part is a pointer directing towards the next node in the linked list.

```
public class Node {
    int data;
    Node next;
}
```

In the class Node, you see the variable data of type int which will hold the data, and 'next' of type Node which will point toward the next node.

One distinguishing characteristic of Linked Lists is the way they are stored in memory. Unlike arrays, nodes are not stored in sequential memory locations; rather, they're scattered throughout memory, and these nodes are connected through links, emphasizing why the pointers play a crucial role in the structure.

A special node, called the HEAD, denotes the starting point of the linked list, and the last node (where the next node is NULL—the node it points to doesn't exist) indicates the end.

2.2. Types of Linked Lists

There are typically three types of linked lists:

1. **Singly Linked List (SLL)**: Every node has data and a 'next' reference, pointing to the next node in the list.

2. **Doubly Linked List (DLL)**: In a DLL, every node has three parts: data, a pointer to the next node, and another pointer to the previous node, thus allowing traversal in both directions.

3. **Circular Linked List**: In a circular linked list, the last node doesn't point to NULL but points back to the HEAD, forming a closed loop.

Your choice of the linked list type depends on the specific requirements of the problem you're trying to solve.

2.3. Operations on a Linked List

Various operations could be performed on a linked list, and understanding each assists in embracing the full functionality of this data structure. These operations typically include:

1. **Traversal**: Walking through each element of the list.

2. **Insertion**: Adding a new node.

3. **Deletion**: Removing a node.

4. **Search**: Finding a node.

Let's detail each operation.

2.3.1. Traversal

Traversal or walking through a linked list involves starting at the head node and moving along the next pointers until you reach a node that points to NULL.

```
public void traverse(Node node) {
    while (node != null) {
        System.out.print(node.data + " ");
        node = node.next;
    }
}
```

This simple function takes the head of the list as an argument and prints out each node's data until the tail.

2.3.2. Insertion

For adding a new node to the linked list, we have three scenarios: inserting at the beginning, at the end, or at a given position.

1. **At the Beginning**: Create a new node, set its next to the current head, and finally update the head to the new node.

2. **At the End**: Traverse the list to the last node, create a new node, and set the next of the last node to the new node.

3. **At a Given Position**: Traverse to the (k-1)th node (1-indexed), create a new node, set the next of the new node to the next of the (k-1)th node, and set the next of the (k-1)th node to the new node.

2.3.3. Deletion

Deleting a node has similar scenarios to insertion. In each case, you'll need to adjust the next pointers so no nodes become lost/unreachable.

1. **From the Beginning**: Set the head to the 2nd node in the list (what the head's next points to).

2. **From the End**: Traverse to the 2nd last node, and set its next to NULL.

3. **From a Given Position**: Traverse to the (k-1)th node, and update the next of the (k-1)th node to the node after its current next.

2.3.4. Search

To find a node with a given data value, you can start at the head and check each node's data. If the wanted value isn't found by the time you reach a node pointing to NULL, it doesn't exist in the list.

```java
public boolean search(Node head, int x)
{
    Node current = head;
    while (current != null)
    {
        if (current.data == x)
            return true;
        current = current.next;
    }
    return false;
}
```

The Time Complexity of traversal, search, insert & delete operations in the linked list is O(n), and the Space Complexity is O(1) for these operations as there is no additional space required.

In conclusion, a solid understanding of linked lists and their operations serves as a basis for grasifying complex data structures. Linked lists play a significant role in data structure and algorithm interviews, and mastering them will be an asset in your journey as a coder. The hands-on approach explained here takes you one step closer to becoming an adept problem solver.

Chapter 3. Distinguishing Singly Linked Lists vs Doubly Linked Lists

Before we dive into distinguishing between singly linked lists and doubly linked lists, it is crucial to understand the concept of a 'node'. A node is the fundamental unit of a linked list, comprising two components - the data and the reference to the next node.

3.1. Structure of Linked Lists

Let's now dissect the core architecture of linked lists. A singly linked list involves each node carrying certain data and pointing to the next node. You can move forward through the links, but reverse navigation is not possible. On the other hand, as the name suggests, a doubly linked list allows navigation in both directions. A node of a doubly linked list consists of three parts: the data, a reference to the next node, and also a link to the previous node.

In terms of depiction, a singly linked list might be visualised as a series of boxes placed linearly, where each box has a specific value and points to the subsequent one. Conversely, a doubly linked list can be imagined as a series of boxes with two arrows stemming out from each, one pointing forward to the next box and the other pointing backward to the previous box.

The final node in both types of lists generally points to NULL, meaning it has no reference to any other node.

3.2. Singly Linked Lists: An Overview

Consider this asciidoc syntax for demonstrating the construction of a singly linked list:

```
public class Node {
    int data;        // Node's data
    Node next;       // Reference to the next node

    // constructor
    Node(int data) {
        this.data = data;
        next = null;
    }
}
```

A singly linked list has several attributes and advantages that make them an appealing choice for many tasks:

1. They are simple to understand and implement.

2. Less memory is used per node because only one link is stored.

3. They can be used to implement data structures like stacks and queues.

However, they also have several substantial limitations:

1. Backward navigation isn't possible.

2. Insertions and deletions at certain positions require the traversal of the entire list from the beginning.

3. Finding the previous element requires additional time, as you must essentially start from the head and navigate until you reach the element before the one of interest.

3.3. Doubly Linked Lists: An Overview

Here is an asciidoc syntax for a doubly linked list's node:

```
public class Node {
    int data;      // Node's data
    Node next;     // Reference to the next node
    Node prev;     // Reference to the previous node

    // constructor
    Node(int data) {
        this.data = data;
        next = prev = null;
    }
}
```

Some key benefits of doubly linked lists include:

1. Backward navigation is made possible.

2. Both next and previous nodes can be accessed directly, which can help in certain algorithms.

3. Insertions and deletions become easier because you don't need to traverse the list from the head to find the previous node.

However, doubly linked lists have some drawbacks:

1. They consume more memory as they use an additional pointer for every node.

2. Implementing them can be a bit more complex as compared to singly linked lists—it requires managing an extra pointer for every operation.

3.4. Singly vs Doubly: Making The Choice

How does one choose between a singly linked list and a doubly linked list? The decision depends largely on your specific needs and resources.

If your task does not require reverse navigation, and memory is a prime concern, a singly linked list would be better suited. However, if you're dealing with more complex use-cases that require traversals in both directions, a doubly linked list could be a more feasible choice.

Your choice will also depend on what your algorithm requires. If you need to access or modify preceding nodes frequently, a doubly linked list would be beneficial, even though it comes with an overhead memory cost. If your algorithm primarily moves forward and requires simpler operations, a singly linked list would be more advantageous.

3.5. Conclusion

Understanding the fundamental differences between singly and doubly linked lists is an integral part of mastering data structures. Determining which type of list to employ is dictated by your application's specific needs and constraints. It is not an 'either-or' situation, but rather a decision of appropriateness. This understanding plays a crucial role in effective problem-solving, algorithm design and ultimately leads to optimised coding solutions.

Through the exploration of these concepts, we hope to bring clarity to the reader and instill them with a deeper understanding of how these data structures function, thereby aiding them in developing intuition to tackle complex coding problems.

Chapter 4. Basics of Linked List Creation and Modification

Linked Lists are a sequential form of data structure, comprising nodes that hold data and pointers connecting these nodes. The nodes hold two fields: data and a reference (or pointer) to the next node in the sequence. In a singly linked list, the link is unidirectional, pointing to the next node. In a doubly linked list, each node has two references pointing to its preceding and succeeding nodes. We will concentrate on singly linked lists, where each node points to its successor and the last node, called tail, points to null value.

4.1. Node and LinkedList Implementation

Before creating a Linked List, it is essential to understand its fundamental building block; the node. A simple node in a Linked List consists of two elements: the data and the link to the next node. Here's how you can design a Node class in Python:

```python
class Node:
    def __init__(self, data=None):
        self.data = data
        self.next = None
```

Here, the Node class contains an initializer (or constructor) that takes a data parameter (default value is None) and assigns it to the data member variable. The next member variable, which will hold the reference to the next node, is also initialized to None.

To create a LinkedList class, we need to initialize the head of our list.

```
class LinkedList:
    def __init__(self):
        self.head = None
```

This simple LinkedList class only contains a single member variable, head, which points towards the first node in the list or None if the list is empty.

4.2. Creating Nodes

Creation of nodes within a linked list would start by building the head node and progressively attaching the following nodes. In the following Python code, we build a LinkedList with three nodes:

```
class Node:
    def __init__(self, data=None):
        self.data = data
        self.next = None

class LinkedList:
    def __init__(self):
        self.head = None

# Instantiate LinkedList
linked_list = LinkedList()

# Create first node and point head towards it
linked_list.head = Node("Head")

# Create second and third nodes
second_node = Node("Second")
third_node = Node("Third")
```

```
# Link first node to second and second to third
linked_list.head.next = second_node
second_node.next = third_node
```

For better readability and reusability, it is recommended to add nodes via a method in the LinkedList class.

4.3. Adding Nodes to LinkedList

Let's include a add method for appending nodes at the end of our list:

```
class LinkedList:
    def __init__(self):
        self.head = None

    def add(self, data):
        if not self.head:
            self.head = Node(data)
        else:
            current_node = self.head
            while current_node.next:
                current_node = current_node.next
            current_node.next = Node(data)

# Create LinkedList and add nodes
linked_list = LinkedList()
linked_list.add("Head")
linked_list.add("Second")
linked_list.add("Third")
```

In the above Python code, we first check if our LinkedList is empty (i.e., head is None). If true, we create a new node and assign it as the head of our list. For a non-empty list, we iterate through the list to find the last node and append a new node to its next member.

4.4. Inserting Nodes at Specific Positions

To assert control over nodes' locations, an insert method enables us to add nodes at specific positions:

```
class LinkedList:
    #... existing methods ...

    def insert(self, data, position):
        new_node = Node(data)

        if position is 0:
            new_node.next = self.head
            self.head = new_node
        else:
            current_node = self.head
            current_position = 0
            while current_node and current_position <
position:
                prev_node = current_node
                current_node = current_node.next
                current_position += 1
            prev_node.next = new_node
            new_node.next = current_node
```

This insert method first checks if the insertion position is at the head. If it's true, it makes the new_node the new head and points its next to the old head. If the position lies within the list, it iterates through the list to find it. The new_node then becomes the next node of the previous node and the current node becomes the next node of new_node.

14

4.5. Removing Nodes

Finally, the `delete` method completes our manipulation basics:

```
class LinkedList:
    #... existing methods ...

    def delete(self, key):
        current_node = self.head
        prev_node = None

        while current_node and current_node.data != key:
            prev_node = current_node
            current_node = current_node.next

        if prev_node is None:
            self.head = current_node.next
        elif current_node:
            prev_node.next = current_node.next
            current_node.next = None
```

In the `delete` method, we first assign head to `current_node` and start traversing our list. If we find our node, we check if it was the head node (prev_node is None). If it was, we set head as the next node, effectively skipping (deleting) the current_node. For a non-head node, we adjust the prev_node's next to skip the `current_node`.

In conclusion, understanding and implementing a linked list, though it might seem complex, forms a fundamental basis for solving even more complex data structures. As we traverse these concepts one step at a time, we understand the underlining principles behind it and develop sound solutions for common problems involving linked lists.

Chapter 5. Traversal Techniques in Linked Lists

Before we immerse ourselves into the various traversal techniques of linked lists, let's first understand what traversal actually means. Traversal, in the realm of data structures, refers to the process of visiting or examining each node (element) stored in a data structure. In the context of linked lists, this means starting at the head (the first node) and following the pointers from one node to the next, ultimately ending up at the tail (the last node).

5.1. Necessity of Traversal

There are many reasons why we might need to traverse a linked list. The most obvious reason is to access the data stored within the list. However, there are many other operations which require traversal, such as finding a specific element, inserting or deleting nodes, or even reversing the list. Without the ability to traverse the list, these operations would be impossible. Therefore, understanding linked list traversal is vital to understanding linked lists themselves.

5.2. Basic Traversal

The simplest traversal technique involves initializing a pointer to the head of the list, then repeatedly moving the pointer to the next node until it remains null, indicating that we have reached the end of the list.

Here's an example in pseudo-code:

```
node = head
while (node != null) {
  print(node.data)
```

```
    node = node.next
}
```

In this example, our loop continues as long as node isn't null. If node does become null, we've reached the end of the list. Inside the loop, we print out the data stored in node (representing the current node we're on), and then move node along to the next node in the list with node = node.next.

This technique is simple yet effective for basic linked list traversal, but there are more specialized techniques for handling different scenarios.

5.3. Two Pointer / Slow-Fast Pointer Technique

This technique utilizes two pointers which move through the list at different speeds. Typically, one pointer ("slow") moves one node at a time, while the other ("fast") moves two nodes at a time. This technique is particularly useful for certain problems, such as detecting cycles in the list or finding the middle element of the list.

Again, here's an example in pseudo-code:

```
slow = head
fast = head
while (fast != null && fast.next != null) {
    slow = slow.next
    fast = fast.next.next
}
```

Upon the loop's termination, the slow pointer would be at the mid-point for an even numbered list, or just past the midpoint for an odd numbered list. This technique works because the fast pointer is moving twice as fast as the slow pointer. So, by the time the fast pointer reaches the end of the list, the slow pointer is only halfway through the list.

5.4. Recursive Traversal

Recursive traversal is another technique to traverse linked lists. However, this method differs from the others because it doesn't use a loop to move through the list. Instead, it uses a function that calls itself with the next node.

Here's an example in pseudo-code:

```
void recursiveTraversal(node)
{
    if (node == null)
    {
        return;
    }
    print(node.data)
    recursiveTraversal(node.next)
}
```

In this example, firstly checks if node is null. If it is, the function returns without doing anything because we've hit the end of the list. If node is not null, it prints the data stored in node, and then calls itself with the next node in the list.

Whilst recursive traversal can be elegant and effective, it's not always the best choice. Due to the recursion stack, it may lead to stack overflow issues for large lists.

5.5. Reverse Traversal

Reverse traversal of a linked list, while not directly possible due to its single direction, can be achieved indirectly through various techniques. One common approach is to first reverse the list using iterative or recursive methods, and then perform the basic traversal on the reversed list. Another common approach is to use a stack to push all nodes of the list and then pop them out, which will result in the nodes being accessed in reverse order.

Here's an example using the reverse-then-traverse approach in pseudo-code:

```
node = head
previous = null
while (node != null)
{
  next = node.next
  node.next = previous
  previous = node
  node = next
}
// 'previous' is now the new head
node = previous
while (node != null)
{
  print(node.data)
  node = node.next
}
```

In this example, first, the list is reversed using a simple three-pointer technique. Then, basic traversal is done on the reversed list.

Understanding and employing these traversing techniques correctly in linked lists can make the process of list handling much easier and cleaner. You'll find that the more you work with linked lists, the more intuitive these methods will become. Happy coding!

Chapter 6. Solving Common Manipulation Challenges

In the practical coding universe, accessing an element directly is a rarity. More often than not, the task lies in manipulation—changing the structure of a linked list in some way or another to solve a particular problem. Let's investigate some common manipulation challenges and unravel strategies to solve these.

6.1. Node Insertion

A relatively straightforward yet important task is inserting a node into a linked list. There are three scenarios where you might need to add a node:

6.1.1. At the Start

Adding a node to the start involves modifying the head of the list. Here is the general approach:

1. Create a new node.

2. Set its next pointer to the current head of the list.

3. Set the list's head to the new node.

Here is how the process would look in pseudocode:

```
function insertAtStart(head, newData):
    newNode = Node(newData)
    newNode.next = head
    head = newNode
    return head
```

6.1.2. At the End

To append a new node to the end of the list, follow these steps:

1. Create a new node.

2. Make the current last node point to the new node.

3. Update the `tail` pointer to point to the new node.

Pseudocode for the above:

```
function insertAtEnd(head, newData):
    newNode = Node(newData)
    if head is None:
        head = newNode
    else:
        last = head
        while last.next is not None:
            last = last.next
        last.next = newNode
    return head
```

6.1.3. In the Middle

Inserting a node in the middle at a given position or just after a given node is a slightly tricky task. Steps include:

1. Create the new node.

2. Set its next pointer to the next pointer of the node after which it is to be placed.

3. Set the next pointer of the previous node to the new node.

Pseudocode isn't much complicated:

```
function insertInMiddle(prevNode, newData):
    if prevNode is None:
        print "Previous node must exist."
        return
    newNode = Node(newData)
    newNode.next = prevNode.next
    prevNode.next = newNode
```

6.2. Node Deletion

One key part of manipulation is node deletion, i.e., removing one or more nodes from the linked list. This can be done in various ways:

6.2.1. Deletion by Key

Here, we're given a key. The node with this key's value is to be deleted. If the key exists in the list, the process involves changing the next pointer of the node previous to the one to be deleted.

Here's the pseudocode:

```
function deleteNodeByKey(head, key):
    temp = head
    if temp is not None:
        if temp.data == key:
            head = temp.next
            temp = None
            return head
    while temp is not None:
        if temp.data == key:
            break
        prev = temp
        temp = temp.next
    if temp == None:
```

```
        return head
    prev.next = temp.next
    temp = None
    return head
```

6.2.2. Deletion by Position

This involves deleting a node at a particular position. If the position exists, we adjust the next pointer of the preceding node to bypass the deleted node.

Here's the pseudocode:

```
function deleteNodeAtPosition(head, position):
    if head == None:
        return
    temp = head
    if position == 0:
        head = temp.next
        temp = None
        return head
    for i in range(0, position - 1):
        temp = temp.next
        if temp is None:
        break
    if temp is None or temp.next is None:
        return head
    next = temp.next.next
    temp.next = None
    temp.next = next
    return head
```

6.3. Linked List Reversal

We'll often come across problems asking us to reverse a linked list. It's a classic problem, with a simple yet elegant solution, requiring the manipulation of next pointers.

Following pseudocode elucidates the approach:

```
function reverseList(head):
    prev = None
    current = head
    while current is not None:
        next = current.next
        current.next = prev
        prev = current
        current = next
    head = prev
    return head
```

That was just the tip of the iceberg. You'll encounter numerous other variations of linked list problems—detecting and removing loops, finding middle elements, merging sorted lists, etc. The key to cracking them lies in the sound understanding of this fundamental data structure. Embrace the manipulation techniques, play with pointers, and you'll start seeing through the problems in no time. Happy Coding!

Chapter 7. Addressing Memory Management in Linked Lists

Let us start off by solidifying our fundamental understanding of Linked Lists. A Linked List, as one may define it, is a linear type of data structure that traverses elements in a sequence. Each element or node holds two types of information - the data and the reference to the next node. Our journey initially shall be focused on memory management, significant to the successful implementation of Linked Lists.

7.1. Memory Allocation

Memory Allocation in a Linked List is typically done dynamically, which greatly reduces memory waste and enhances efficiency. The strategy is, basically, allocating memory whenever necessary and freeing it when it is no longer required. This dynamic nature of memory allocation sets Linked Lists apart from their static counterparts like arrays.

In languages such as C and C++, memory allocation is achieved using built-in functions such as `malloc()`, `calloc()`, and `free()`. Here's a basic example of how one would newly allocate a node in C:

```
struct Node* newNode = (struct
Node*)malloc(sizeof(struct Node));
```

In contrast, higher-level languages like Python and Java handle memory allocation automatically when a new object (node) is created. However, understanding the principles of dynamic memory allocation remains crucial regardless of your primary programming language.

7.2. Dealing with Memory Leaks

One notorious drawback of dynamic memory allocation is the possibility of memory leaks. This manifestation occurs when the program doesn't free the memory that is no longer required. In other words, the memory, once allocated, never gets deallocated if not explicitly treated causing a drain of memory resources.

One such situation in Linked Lists is when a node gets detached from the list but not deallocated. This problem is particularly acute in languages like C/C++ where memory management is a manual process.

To prevent such issues, it is essential to free a node when it is removed from the list.

7.3. Handling Dangling Pointers

In the context of Linked Lists, a dangling pointer can occur when a node is removed. Without correct pointer management, the pointer which previously pointed to the removed node could end up pointing to an undefined memory location. This could lead to unpredictable behavior in the program.

Proper pointer management essentials include:

1. Nullifying the pointer after freeing the node it points to.
2. Making sure no other pointers are still pointing to the freed node.

In C++ and other languages that allow pointer manipulation, these practices should be thoroughly implemented to avoid logical errors and crashes.

For instance, to delete a node in a singly linked list, we can't directly free the node as we must ensure its previous node points to its next node. Here's a brief C++ snippet showing how:

```cpp
void deleteNode(Node **head_ref, int key) {
    Node* temp = *head_ref;
    Node* prev = NULL;

    if (temp != NULL && temp->data == key)     // If head
node holds the key
    {
        *head_ref = temp->next;
        delete temp;
        temp = NULL;
        return;
    }

    else
    {
        while (temp != NULL && temp->data != key)
        {
            prev = temp;
            temp = temp->next;
        }
        if (temp == NULL) return;    // If key was not
present in linked list

        prev->next = temp->next;
        delete temp;
        return;
    }
}
```

7.4. Utilizing Memory Efficiently

Leveraging memory to its utmost capacity is undoubtfully advantageous. Despite this, Linked Lists are often criticized for their higher memory use compared to adjacent data structures like arrays. This is because of the need to store the pointer to the next node in each item of the list.

Nevertheless, the splurge on space is justified when flexibility and frequent 'deletion-insertion' operations are paramount. Care must be taken, though, to ensure that the extra memory used does not become a bottleneck. Employing techniques such as shared pointers in doubly linked lists can help in efficiently using the memory.

7.5. Garbage Collection

For those using high-level languages like Java and Python, garbage collection comes into play, offering a great boon. This automatically reclaims the memory which is no longer in use or needed. The garbage collector keeps track of all objects in memory and discerns those no longer accessible by the program. It eliminates such objects, freeing up memory space. While this does not eliminate the need for good memory management practices, it can significantly lessen the burden and risk of memory leaks.

7.6. Conclusion

Wrapped up within this seemingly simple structure of Linked Lists, we find a plethora of intricacies related to memory management. Dynamic allocation, the concept of dangling pointers and memory leaks, memory efficiency, as well as garbage collection, are each integral to operational understanding, no matter what programming language one chooses to work with. As we journey further onwards into the realm of complex coding challenges, this mastery of Linked

Lists and associated memory management will prove instrumental in developing robust code and efficient solutions.

Chapter 8. Cyclic Linked Lists: Identification and Resolution

To begin our exploration of cyclic linked lists, we must first understand the basic structure of a linked list. It is a collection of nodes, where each node has two components: a 'data' element that contains the actual information and a 'next' element that points to the next node in the sequence. In a cyclic linked list, the 'next' pointer of the last node points back to an earlier node, creating a loop.

8.1. Understanding a Cyclic Linked List

A cyclic linked list is quite similar to a regular linked list, with one crucial difference: in a regular or "linear" linked list, the last node's 'next' points to null, indicating the end of the list. On the contrary, in a cyclic linked list, the last node's 'next' points back to any node in the list, violating the linear progression.

The head of a cyclic linked list can be anywhere within the cycle. It might be on the node which initiates the cycle, or it could be somewhere before the cycle starts. The point to note here is, traversing a cyclic linked list would result in an infinite loop. Therefore, detection whether a linked list has a cycle is paramount.

Firstly, to understand why cyclic linked lists occur, we need to ascertain potential reasons. Commonly they arise due to coding errors or logical mistakes where pointers are incorrectly managed.

8.2. Detecting a Cyclic Linked List

Attempting to detect whether a linked list contains a cycle is one of the primary challenges programmers face when working with this data structure. Many algorithms are in use for this purpose; however, Floyd's Cycle-Finding Algorithm (or better known as the Hare and Tortoise algorithm) is one of the more popular and efficient ones.

This algorithm involves two pointers that traverse the list at different speeds. Typically, the 'hare' moves at double the speed of the 'tortoise.' If a cycle exists, the hare will eventually lap the tortoise (they will land on the same node). Conversely, if no cycle exists, the hare will reach the end of the list (a null node).

Here is a basic implementation of this method in pseudocode:

```
[listing]
```

initialize pointer1 and pointer2 at the head node while pointer2 is not null and pointer2.next is not null: move pointer1 ahead by one node move pointer2 ahead by two nodes if pointer1 == pointer2: return True # cycle detected return False # cycle not detected

```
[listing]
```

8.3. Fixing a Cyclic Linked List

After identifying a cyclic linked list, the next challenge is to resolve it. In other words, the challenge is to convert a cyclic linked list back into a regular, linear linked list.

The primary step in resolving a cycle involves identifying the node where the cycle begins. This is carried out by keeping the hare pointer static after the previous step and moving the tortoise pointer back to the head. Then, both pointers are moved forward at the same speed until they meet, which will be the start of the loop.

The algorithm to solve the cycle then looks like this:

```
[listing]
```

assuming the cycle has been detected and hare and tortoise meet at a node

move tortoise back to the head node while tortoise is not equal to hare: move hare and tortoise ahead by one node each # when they meet again, the node is the cycle's starting point

to remove the cycle, find the last node in cycle

while hare.next is not equal to tortoise: move hare ahead by one node # set hare's next node to null hare.next = null

```
[listing]
```

Though this seems like a lengthy process, it's quite efficient as it traverses the linked list in O(n) time complexity and uses O(1) auxiliary space.

In conclusion, working with cyclic linked lists presents specific challenges. From identification to resolution, each step requires a strong understanding of the data structure and the logic behind it. As with all things in the coding domain, practice is crucial. Implement these algorithms, understand their flow, and develop your version to face any problem related to cyclic linked lists with confidence.

Chapter 9. Complex Challenges: Reversing Linked Lists

Depending on your grasp of the fundamental concepts about linked lists, reversing a linked list could be an exciting challenge or a daunting task. However, armed with the basics well etched in your memory, you'd find unraveling this problem piece-by-piece quite enthralling.

9.1. Understanding the Problem

The basic challenge here is to reverse the order of elements in a linked list. Consider a linked list: $1 \rightarrow 2 \rightarrow 3 \rightarrow 4 \rightarrow 5 \rightarrow$ NULL. The goal is to make it $5 \rightarrow 4 \rightarrow 3 \rightarrow 2 \rightarrow 1 \rightarrow$ NULL. Seems simple, right? Let's dive into the solution.

9.2. Iterative Approach

One way we can tackle this problem is by using an iterative approach. The general principle behind this approach is traversing the nodes of the original linked list one by one while changing the `next` node of each node to point to its previous node.

To perform this operation, we'll need to keep track of three items at each step: the current node, the previous node, and the next node. Let's try to visualize the process:

Original Linked List: $1 \rightarrow 2 \rightarrow 3 \rightarrow 4 \rightarrow 5 \rightarrow$ NULL

Iteration 1: NULL $\leftarrow 1$ $2 \rightarrow 3 \rightarrow 4 \rightarrow 5 \rightarrow$ NULL

Here, 1 has been detached from 2. The pointer from 1 now points to

NULL (as 1 is the new end of the reversed linked list) as 2, 3, 4, 5 are waiting to be reversed.

This process is repeated until all nodes have been traversed, reversing their direction.

Iteration 2: NULL ← 1 ← 2 3 → 4 → 5 → NULL

Iteration 3: NULL ← 1 ← 2 ← 3 4 → 5 → NULL

Iteration 4: NULL ← 1 ← 2 ← 3 ← 4 5 → NULL

Iteration 5: NULL ← 1 ← 2 ← 3 ← 4 ← 5 NULL

And voila, you've got your reversed linked list!

Here is what the Python programming language sample code for this iterative method looks like:

```python
def reverseIteratively(head):

    prev_node = None
    curr_node = head

    while curr_node:
        next_node = curr_node.next
        curr_node.next = prev_node
        prev_node = curr_node
        curr_node = next_node

    return prev_node
```

This method has a time complexity of O(n) and a space complexity of O(1) as it involves a single traversal of the linked list and uses only a constant amount of space.

9.3. Recursive Approach

An elegant and succinct approach to this problem uses recursion. The idea with this approach is that we want to change the next of our current node to point to the previous one. But how can we change the next of a node if we haven't processed the following nodes yet?

The answer is recursion. Recursive solutions are often straightforward, as they turn the problem into a similar problem of smaller size. The reversal of the entire list is trivial once we've reversed the remaining part of the list.

Given the linked list $1 \rightarrow 2 \rightarrow 3 \rightarrow 4 \rightarrow 5 \rightarrow$ NULL, our task is to transform it into NULL $\leftarrow 1 \leftarrow 2 \leftarrow 3 \leftarrow 4 \leftarrow 5$. Once we've transformed the linked list into NULL $\leftarrow 2 \leftarrow 3 \leftarrow 4 \leftarrow 5$, it's easy to just attach 1 at the end (1 follows NULL after reversal).

The termination condition is when we have no more nodes left in the original linked list (i.e., we've consumed all the nodes and reversed all the directive pointers),"node == NULL".

In Python, this would look as:

```python
def reverseRecursively(node):

    if not node or not node.next:
        return node

    p = reverseRecursively(node.next)
    node.next.next = node
    node.next = None

    return p
```

This method also has time complexity O(n) comparable to the

iterative approach. The space complexity is O(n) due to recursive stack space usage.

9.4. Wrap Up

It's crucial to choose the right approach based on the situation — while recursion may offer a more elegant and shorter solution, it also uses more memory. On the other hand, iteration can save memory, but it might be more involved.

These two solutions present different ways to solve the reverse-a-linked-list problem—a common challenge that underlines the importance of mastering linked lists. Implementing solutions to problems like these apart from being a strong introduction to essential concepts associated with linked lists, also cultivates structured thinking, meticulous analysis, and proficient problem-solving. Sail over these challenges, and harness a better understanding and command over linked lists!

Chapter 10. Utilizing Linked Lists in Real-world Scenarios

Linked lists, as you've now come to understand in the previous chapters, are not just an interesting data structure but also a highly useful computer science tool. The flexibility that linked lists provide is unparalleled. They not only extend intuitive coding options but also give an efficient approach to manage data. Now that you've learned and practiced many examples of coding with linked lists, let us dig deeper in order to understand their utility in real-world problems.

Data structures are seldom used directly; more often, they're integrated in algorithms or systems to solve complex problems in real-life scenarios. Let's discuss how linked lists are implemented in applications with unique requirements.

10.1. Assisting Garbage Collection

Garbage collection is a form of automatic memory management that attempts to reclaim garbage or memory that's no longer in use by the program. Some garbage collection algorithms, like Mark-and-Sweep, use linked lists to keep track of objects waiting to be cleaned up.

Take an example. You have been asked to develop a system memory manager with garbage collection capabilities. A singly linked list becomes a natural choice to maintain a list of memory blocks. Each node would be analogous to a block of memory and can contain information about the memory block, such as its size, usage status, or location. The linked list helps maintain a dynamic structure, that can add or remove memory block data as per system requirements.

10.2. Memory Management

In areas where memory usage needs to be optimized, linked lists can play a vital role. For instance, when implementing a hash map, collision handling via chaining can be efficiently handled using linked lists.

Consider the situation where you need to develop an application that handles extensive data. Here, efficiency becomes critical, especially when it comes to memory management. Using hashes to directly access data can save time, but dealing with collisions could create hurdles. Chaining solves this issue by using a linked list to store collided data, allowing it to grow or shrink based on the data it needs to store.

10.3. Symbol Table Construction in Compilers

In the field of compiler design, linked lists serve as the backbone of symbol table structure. The symbol table is a fundamental part of a compiler. Its function is to store the identifiers present in the source program, each associated with relevant information.

In the process of constructing a compiler, managing value assignation and data manipulations become easier if you employ a doubly linked list. It allows backtracking, fetching data values, and maintaining records of various identifiers with ease.

10.4. Undo Functionality

Linked lists impact our lives in everyday applications as well. Think of the undo functionality - a linked list stores actions performed, facilitating the ability to revert the state of an application to any previous point in time.

When designing software that needs to provide an undo feature, a natural choice would be a doubly linked list, as it allows users to traverse backwards in the list, and revert actions accordingly. This functionality provides powerful capabilities to end users, from undoing text editing in word processors to reverting complex moves in game applications.

10.5. Gaussian Elimination

Linked lists also find application in mathematical computations. One such example is the Gaussian elimination method to solve linear equations. Using linked lists for the representation and manipulation of sparse matrices can save both space and computing time.

When tasked with designing a system to handle extensive mathematical computations like the Gaussian elimination, a linked list based structure could become essential. It enables managing sparse matrices, saving vital memory and execution time for other complex computations.

10.6. Music Player

In the world of entertainment, modern music players use linked lists to manage songs in a playlist. The next and the previous pointer enable easy navigation through a playlist.

Suppose you are creating a music app, and you need to manage a user's playlist. Using a doubly linked list can facilitate moving to the next or previous song, deleting a song, or adding a new song in between, thus enhancing the user's experience.

Whilst the above examples discuss only a few real-world applications, linked lists serve a plethora of purposes across varied domains. Understanding their underlying principles and gaining practice with their implementation can prepare you to harness their potential fully. Tackle challenging problems, find optimal solutions, and make your code more efficient with linked lists. Staying open to learning is key. Continue this journey of exploring data structures, and you'll enhance your potential as a coder, problem solver, and innovator in this digital era.

Chapter 11. Coding Interview Questions and Their Solutions: A Deep Dive

In the coding world, the importance of deep understanding can't be overstressed when it comes to resolving challenges, especially those posed during technical interviews. Bearing this in mind, we focus this chapter on spotlighting types of questions you might encounter and demonstrating their solutions, progressively from simple to more complex scenarios. Our emphasis will be primarily on the Linked List data structure.

11.1. Understanding Linked Lists

A linked list is a linear data structure in which each element is a separate object. Each element (which we will refer to as a node) contains two items: the data and a reference (aka link) to the next node in the sequence. This structure permits efficient insertion or removal of elements from any position in the sequence during iteration.

Let's see a graphical illustration:

```
[ data | next ] --> [ data | next ] --> [ data | next ]
--> NULL
```

Here every 'data' represents the data stored in the node, and 'next' is a pointer that points to the next node in the list. The last node, as you can see, points to NULL indicating the end of the list.

11.2. Basic Operations on Linked Lists

Linked Lists have several common operations:

1. **Insertion** – Adds an element at the beginning of the list.

2. **Deletion** – Deletes an element from the list using the key.

3. **Search** – Searches an element using the given key.

4. **Indexing** – Accesses element from the list using an index number.

11.3. Common Interview Questions On Linked Lists

Now, let's dive into some common interview questions and their solutions:

1) How to find the middle of a linked list in one pass?

The classic approach to this problem employs what we call the "two-pointer" technique. Basically, you have two pointers, where one moves twice as fast as the other. When the faster pointer reaches the end of the list, the slower pointer will be at the midpoint.

```
def findMiddle(head):
    slow_ptr = head
    fast_ptr = head

    if head is not None:
        while(fast_ptr is not None and fast_ptr.next is
not None):
            fast_ptr = fast_ptr.next.next
            slow_ptr = slow_ptr.next
```

```
    return slow_ptr
```

2) How to detect if a linked list has a cycle?

The 'Floyd's Cycle-Finding' algorithm is an optimized approach, also based on the two-pointer strategy. In it, two pointers move at different speeds (one twice as fast as the other). If there's a loop, they'll meet; if not, the faster pointer will reach the end.

```
def hasLoop(head):
    slow = head
    fast = head
    while(slow and fast and fast.next):
        slow = slow.next              #moves one step at
a time
        fast = fast.next.next         #moves two steps at
a time

        if slow == fast:              #loop exists
            return True

    return False                      #loop doesn't exist
```

3) How to reverse a linked list?

Reversing a linked list can be achieved by initializing three pointers: the previous node, the current node, and the next node. When the current node is the head, the previous node is NULL. We iterate across the linked list, moving the 'next node' pointer to the next node, reversing the current node's next pointer, and then pushing the 'previous node' and 'current node' pointers one step forward.

```
def reverse(head):
```

```
    prev_node = None
    current_node = head
    while(current_node is not None):
        next_node = current_node.next
        current_node.next = prev_node
        prev_node = current_node
        current_node = next_node
    return prev_node
```

These succinctly explained problems and solutions serve as the bedrock for understanding diverse interview questions based on Linked Lists. As you grow more comfortable with the operation of Linked Lists, and the fundamental logic behind using them, more complex questions will seem less daunting and easier to tackle. This knowledge is a robust tool in your interview preparation arsenal, that can bestow on you a significantly strong edge over your competitors. Don't forget the key here is practice and understanding, so keep practicing, and happy coding!

www.ingramcontent.com/pod-product-compliance
Lightning Source LLC
LaVergne TN
LVHW051622050326
832903LV00033B/4620